PETER LODATO

From Installation to Painting

D1232799

Selected Works from 1980 to 2000

FREDERICK R. WEISMAN MUSEUM OF ART

Pepperdine University

Introduction

This mid-career survey of the Los Angeles artist Peter Lodato was organized to reexamine a body of work that has not received the attention it deserves. The American art world at the opening of the twenty-first century is a rich, inclusive field of vital activity. Los Angeles in particular has seen phenomenal growth in the last two decades, rising from a regional art center to one of international importance. Yet despite the scope of the contemporary art world—and despite the breath of critical attention that accompanies it—certain artists have been overlooked. One of these is Peter Lodato.

Peter Lodato began making work in the late 1960s as part of the California Light and Space movement. Since that time he has developed a body of work of admirable depth and complexity. In the 1970s, and in the wake of Minimalism, his art was openly admired and celebrated. Reviewing a 1975 installation, Fidel Danieli, who for a time was West Coast editor of *Artforum*, wrote that he "was tempted to suggest that [Lodato] is one of the major southern California artists to emerge in the 1970s."[1]

Then the 1980s arrived. The new decade saw the rise of stridently Postmodern styles such as Neo-expressionism and appropriation, which quickly overshadowed earlier movements, making a purist art of perception seem insignificant by comparison. When Lodato was featured at the 1981 Whitney Biennial, his minimalist wall installation was singled out as an oddity, as the sole attempt to sustain an aesthetic of understatement that was being overshadowed by more flamboyant and energetic artworks.[2] Rather than question the direction of his art—as many artists do when faced with a radical shift in period taste—Lodato stuck to his vision and refined it over the years.

It is ironic that the rise of Postmodernism, which led to Lodato's initial neglect, produced a new critical perspective that now allows for a positive reevaluation of his art. Postmodernism sought to question traditional theories of knowledge by deconstructing topics previously thought to be beyond question. Vision, which for centuries was assumed to be a neutral and transparent window onto the world, was now seen as a complex enterprise influenced by such factors as the intent and identity of the observer. New terms of inquiry arose, focusing on the social framework of vision. In light of this new emphasis on critically examining the parameters of sight, Peter Lodato's art—particularly because of the way he "pictures" social space—seems timely and relevant once again.

As a curator relatively new to Los Angeles, I was unaware of Lodato's art during the heyday of the Light and Space movement, when it was receiving the most attention. When I became acquainted with his work a few years ago, I was able to see it with fresh eyes, unbiased by the rhetoric of the 1970s. It is my hope that the qualities and issues I perceived in the art come through in this exhibition and in my essay for the exhibition catalogue.

Michael Zakian
Director
FREDERICK R. WEISMAN MUSEUM OF ART

1 Fidel Danieli, "Painterly Experiences," *Artweek*, 20 December 1975, p. 5.
2 Robert Hughes, "Art: Quirks, Clamors and Variety," *Time*, 2 March 1981, p. 84.

Peter Lodato and *Zuikan*, 1985, oil and wax on canvas over panel, 96 × 96 inches, collection of The Capital Group Foundation

Vision and Violence

"A painter's world is a visible world, nothing but visible: a world almost demented because it is complete when it is yet only partial. Painting awakens and carries to its highest pitch a delirium which is vision itself, for to see is to have at a distance; painting spreads this strange possession to all aspects of Being, which must in some fashion become visible in order to enter into the work of art."

Maurice Merleau-Ponty[1]

"Every human act is an act of violence."

Barnett Newman[2]

Since 1970, Peter Lodato's art has consistently examined the relationship of people to physical space. Strongly influenced by the California Light and Space movement of the late 1960s and early 1970s, his work ostensibly explores expanse and illumination. Yet this obvious interest in glowing light and sparse geometric form are a small facet of his art. Like other artists of the Postminimalist generation, Lodato set out to reinvigorate minimal form and find new life in barren geometry. He came to focus on psychic space, on space as perceived and inhabited by human subjects. His paintings are about the reflexivity of this lived space; about the way we subdivide and compartmentalize our lives and environment, both physically and psychologically. Lodato's ideal is the clean, well-lighted room. How he pictures this arena—how he articulates its borders and delineates its parameters—offers a revealing insight into the conditions of both art and life in America in the last quarter of the twentieth century.

In his own way Lodato has remade modernism in the wake of its demise. Rather than turn to the stereotyped forms of Postmodern discourse—appropriated imagery, linguistic tropes, and ironic parody—he found renewed significance in the modernist vocabulary of purist, reductive forms. By probing the inherent social implications of rational geometry, he has effected his own postmodern revolution, discovering holes in the modernist project and revealing their deeper implications. The great rupture he probes centers around that familiar but curious phenomenon—the rectilinear room. We live in a starkly geometric world of our own making. The implications of our blind dependence on geometry form a vital thread in Lodato's work.

One important and often overlooked theme in his seemingly passive art is violence—and the complex relationship of violence to vision. As Merleau-Ponty noted in *The Primary of Perception*, vision is paradoxical, promising nothing less than the "world" yet remaining frustratingly "partial." For all its capacity to transcend the material, vision remains limited by real physical conditions. This gap between what vision promises and what it actually yields is disappointing and baffling—or, to use Merleau-Ponty's term, "demented." It is a source of the world's violence. Lodato always admired the art of Barnett Newman and agrees with his observation that a certain brutality pervades all aspects of life. Even when things seem tranquil and benign, there is a conflict inherent in the very act of being alive. Lodato's concern with world's latent violence appears most clearly in his use of geometry. While we tend to associate geometry with ideal reason, it also involves a vicious reshaping of natural materials into something unrealistically perfect. When used in his art, Lodato reveals geometry to be beautiful and serene but also harsh and cruel.

Peter Lodato was born in 1946 in Los Angeles to Carlo Lodato, a film editor, and Margaret, née Gretel-Royce, a native of Vienna. Raised in Van Nuys in the San Fernando Valley, he was introduced to art by his mother who showed him books on art and took him to museums. He enrolled as an undergraduate at San Fernando Valley State College, now California State University, Northridge, originally planning to major in psychology. After being introduced to art history, he switched his major to art, and received his B.A. in 1969. He remained at the school for a few more years, continuing graduate studies in art through 1971.

Lodato's years at Cal State Northridge in the late 1960s corresponded to a turning point in American art. In the last years of the 1960s, the absolute authority of geometric styles based on Minimalism and Hardedge abstraction began to wane. A new complex phenomena arose which sought "the dematerialization of the art object," to use Lucy Lippard's phrase. Artists began to question the hegemony of all integral art objects—both avant-garde and traditional—as signs of an overly materialistic and authoritarian society. Instead of manufacturing objects, they began making art based on concepts, processes or systems of information, creating such movements as Conceptual Art, Process Art, and Earth Art. Though still a student Lodato assimilated the ethos of the Postminimalist generation, which saw art as an idealistic mode of free experimentation. As an undergraduate he produced competent but derivative abstract paintings—based on the shaped canvases of Ron Davis and Frank Stella—but soon rejected the entire enterprise, recalling that he "wanted to get as far away from painting as possible."

He abandoned traditional easel painting with a series of shelf constructions of around 1969, which he considers to be his first mature works. Drawing upon the precedent of Donald Judd's metal and Plexiglas primary objects, these long, narrow sheet metal shelves were hung to create a horizontal line at eye level. A coat of paint on the upper surface reflected a colored light on the wall above, while its mass cast a shadow below. Lodato explained that what he "wanted to do was to make a literal illusion . . . That's why I made those shelves . . . I wanted illusion that was totally verifiable, that wasn't a magic trick." [3]

Illusion became one of the key elements of Lodato's art. He was fascinated by illusion because he believes in the supremacy of vision. A highly visual person, he feels that seeing is the primary sense, the principal way we learn about reality. He is drawn to vision because of its immediacy and its breadth—its efficiency and accessibility. By using the eyes, even the most remote object is readily brought into the fold of consciousness. But vision is far from perfect. Lodato knows that vision offers truth, but also error. It can deceive as much as reveal. He wanted "literal illusion" because he wanted his art to reveal the paradoxical nature of human perception, exposing the fact that perception is always uncertain and illusory.

This concern with illusion, which runs throughout the artist's work, also must be seen in the context of his times. In the late 1960s the United States saw the rise of a large and vehement anti-war movement. Protests against the Vietnam War promoted the perception that the government was dishonest. Numerous young people saw America as having institutionalized deceit. Like many of his generation, Lodato subconsciously responded to this situation by embracing deception. At a time when government lies were presented as truth, many artists reacted by making factual truths that were themselves visual lies. By incorporating illusion into his work, Lodato triumphed over falsehood. His shelves rendered deception in an aesthetic form, as a quiet protest against a world ruled by lies.

After the shelves, Lodato moved further away from painting by abandoning the art object and creating light installations. He made light sculptures using only a 2000-watt lamp set on the floor and a mirror to create a light environment. The mirror served a dual role of reflector and obstacle, spreading the light on its polished surface and creating a dark shadow immediately behind. By carefully choosing its angle, the mirror reflected a column of light that illuminated the room but also cut into it. These light and mirror installations were about making and breaking. They reveal the emergence of an important dualistic element in Lodato's art, an appreciation for phenomena that is both constructive and destructive.

While intriguing, these light installations seemed too indefinite and were soon abandoned. Lodato saw a way of replacing these geometric patterns of light with rectangular shapes spray-painted directly on the wall. Still suspicious of the conservative qualities of traditional paint, he turned to Murano pigment, which was colorless but iridescent. This eccentric industrial material—which reveals the artist's affinity with the California Fetish Finish movement—produced different coloristic effects as a viewer passed in front of it. These Murano wall paintings—which Lodato produced from 1971 to 1973—were given life by the active presence of the viewer in the room. Important to Lodato's development was the fact that in the Murano wall installations, paint was used for "manipulating zones in a room spatially."[4] The art drew attention to the viewer's physical place in the room.

Because they were so ethereal, the Murano wall paintings failed to keep the artist's interest. After a friend remarked that they did not reflect the artist's own forceful personality, Lodato soon switched to traditional pigmented paint. He returned to color, not for its decorative value, but because of its psychodynamic resonance. He became fascinated by the projective quality of color, by the fact that a pigment "would push the space in and out."[5] This talk of push and pull harks back to Hans Hofmann, but while the Abstract Expressionist was referring to the active juxtaposition of dramatically contrasting colors, Lodato was interested in the psychophysical qualities of one single color. When a critic reviewed an installation and observed that a large purple rectangle "alternately makes an optical hole in the wall, then seems to float out in front a couple of inches," he grasped the artist's intent.[6] This sense of muscular pulse, of a form actively breathing in and out, was exactly what Lodato wanted.

One of his first public installations using pigmented paint was executed at the University of California, Irvine in 1975. It consisted of a looming black rectangle, painted directly upon the wall, juxtaposed with a similar shape in white. Despite the similarity in size and shape, there were many subtle differences between the two rectangles. The black was richly matte, which contrasted with the reflective gloss white. They also differed in depth. The white rectangle was painted upon Sheetrock, which projected about an inch in front of the wall, creating ambiguities between substance and surface.

At the time, Fidel Danieli wrote that the Irvine installation provided "fresh interpretations of ideas of scale, use of color and color optics, objecthood, viewing

opposite
FOUR STUDIES FOR INSTALLATIONS
1989
Graphite on paper
30 × 22 1/2 inches (each)
Collection of Joseph and Courtney Price,
Washington D.C.

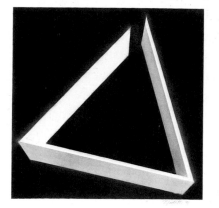 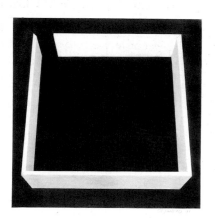

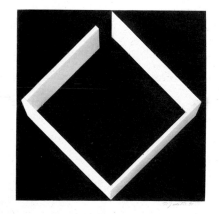 

distance and viewer motion. In content they deal with the contrast of a painter's energy engaged in works of a large (eleven-foot) size and the disarming familiarity and quiet authority of the results. They also concern the conflict of a flat-out geometric simplicity with the ambiguities of possible readings, retinal changes and levels of interpretation. They explore the difference between 'knowing' and 'seeing'." [7]

In an effort to offer his own explanations for his art, Lodato turned to various rationales, typically contrasting a quietist reading with a more forceful interpretation. For example he discussed the overwhelming luminosity of white in terms of Zen transcendence. It was pure and immaculate, an impeccable vision of ideal perfection. Yet to explain the contrast between black and white, he resorted to the more active language of alchemy. He noted that the disparity between black and white reflects alchemical notions of violent transformation with white referring to transcendent purity, black signifying decay and putrefaction.

Through the late 1970s and 1980s, Lodato produced numerous wall installations. Designed for specific spaces, they all explored different spatial relationships within the interior. Often the size and placement of the rectangles mirrored the dimensions and proportions of the room, cutting spaces into visual halves. In these acts of constructive deconstruction, the whole is revealed to be nothing more than a sum of individual parts. The *Otis/Parsons Installation* (1982) consisted of two pairs of rectangles, one pair painted in black and white, the other pair rendered in a near white (pale pink) and a near black (dark green). This work tested the range of human color perception.

An important installation was *La Mer* (1985) executed at the La Jolla Museum of Contemporary Art, now the San Diego Museum of Contemporary Art. It consisted of two horizontal plaster planes, each measuring sixty-three inches high and sixteen feet wide, set to form a juncture in one corner of the gallery. He left one panel plain white plaster, the other he painted deep violet. These synthetic colors turned the viewer's attention back to himself and to his place within the gallery. To deepen the observer's self-awareness, Lodato set the horizontal edge of each panel at the eye-height of the average viewer. The top of each Sheetrock plane was covered with gold leaf that produced a subtle glow of reflected light on the white wall above it. This halo of golden light marked the horizon as something both real and emphatic but also distant and illusory.

Lodato saw the horizon line in transcendental terms. Since it lay beyond one's reach it seemed to represent a timeless, inaccessible realm. He once explained

12

opposite
LA MER
1991
Watercolor on paper
28 x 28 inches
Collection of Elizabeth F. Kitchen

14

his installations by referring to experiences he had on a beach in Malibu as a young man. He was moved by the complex visual sensations "that happen there, because of the sunsets on the water, the reflections, because of the overcast and haze."[8] Despite the fullness of sensation, his final impression was that of a void, of an alluring emptiness. His imagination was continually drawn to that curious point on the horizon "that exists beyond where the water meets the land—a whole world that you cannot walk into, that you can't permeate—that just exists out there." In installations such as *La Mer*, he tried to duplicate that feeling "of perceiving something so vast that you can't step into."

Art historian Robert Rosenblum coined the phrase "Abstract Sublime" to refer to this reverential awe for the elemental vastness of nature. He originally employed the term in order to explain how the immense, indefinite Abstract Expressionist paintings by Barnett Newman, Mark Rothko and Clyfford Still could inspire sublime feelings. Although Lodato drew upon this aesthetic, he avoided falling prey to a simplistic nature mysticism. In fact, while he was inspired by perceptions of the real world, he wanted his installations to have their own internal logic and intellectual rigor. For example, he purposefully avoided colors such as blue and green which have clear associations to nature beyond the gallery walls: "My feeling about color is not to allude to some kind of world conception, but to stimulate perception, to produce a physiological response within the nature of seeing. It is important to me that the color be synthetic, and have a physiological identity rather than one that alludes to nature."[9]

When he wasn't producing wall installations, Lodato would make drawings as plans for possible installations. After his friend, the artist Tom Wudl, commented that they would make great paintings, Lodato began to create imaginary architectural interiors as independent works of art. Originally these dry, descriptive plans were stark and diagrammatic, typical of the 1970s Postminimalist trend towards art as information. As Lodato developed these drawings into paintings, they became more complicated and illusionistic. He began to incorporate real sensory phenomena such as the play of light and shadow upon imaginary walls. His renderings went from the mechanical to the sensuous. As Lodato focused on the lush qualities of light, the cold hard facts of an architectural plan acquired the resonance of a living, breathing environment. Light not only fell upon white walls, but bounced throughout the space, casting shadows and reflecting off surfaces.

15

As seen in *Ruins* (1984), *Red Room* (1985), and *Taukin* (1986), these oil paintings of fanciful architectural interiors continue his life-long concern with light, color and the uncertainty of human perception. But they also address a new issue—the room. No longer simply about human perception, they now examine the social construction of living space. His art became a meditation on the geometric enclosures in which we all live and work. These common everyday spaces, cubic and compartmentalized, define the core of our built environment and reveal much about contemporary America's beliefs and values.

As in his wall installations, these architectural interiors are pure, white and seemingly tranquil. An even, transcendental light permeates the scene, bathing everything in a uniform glow. Yet despite the attempt to render the feel of an actual place, these interiors are patent fictions. Lacking a roof and made of walls that are paper thin, they are as false as studio props, as insubstantial as stage sets. Lodato's immaterial walls are postindustrial and in this sense, Postmodern. They also allude to a Westernized version of a traditional Japanese interior—a simple, sparse aesthetic space that stands for understated elegance. Yet despite this apparent calm, his rooms convey a mood of unease and disquiet. This latent anxiety is conveyed by the unnatural precision of his interior spaces, by their stark artificiality and by their curious distortion of space.

The fictional rooms reveal how much our interiors are dominated and controlled by geometry. Lodato first turned to geometry in order to celebrate austere precision. He wanted a fineness of detail, and a faultless refinement of edge. As a result these interiors are slightly surreal in the way they offer a field of vision that is sharper and more exacting than what we would normally perceive. But what is sacrificed is the human element. It is worth remembering that ancient Greek architecture introduced minor but telling deviations from a strict mathematical scheme—such as the swelling of columns known as entasis—in order to create a building that appeared as an integrated organism. The ancients wanted a structure that had the reflexivity of a living thing. Lodato's geometry remains rigid and stolid, a sign of forces that lay beyond our control—much like our constructed environment.

The massive development of America in the last half-century has brought a new type of inexpensive construction based on the economic use of geometric components. Rather than shape buildings to suit human needs, developers built

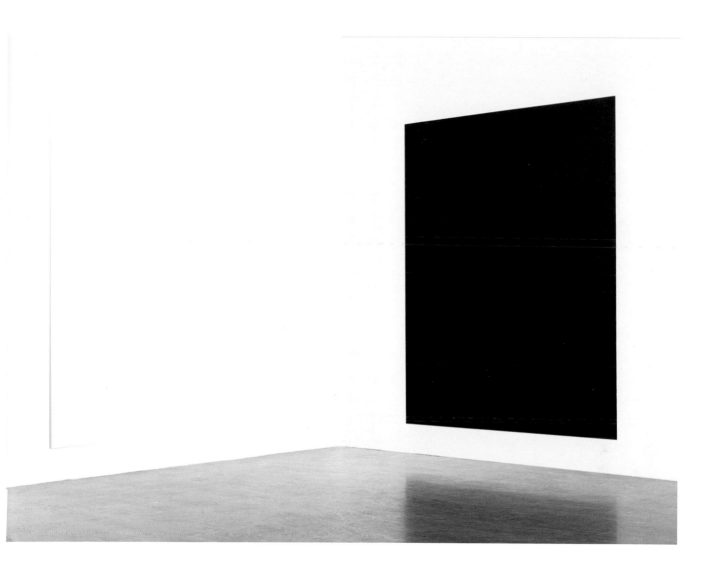

OTIS / PARSONS INSTALLATION
1982
Plaster and enamel
132 × 96 inches (each rectangle)
Collection of the artist

LA MER
La Jolla Museum of Contemporary Art Installation
1985
Plaster, flashe and gold leaf
63 × 384 × 1 1/2 inches
Collection of the artist

OPEN TRIANGLE
Mattress Factory Installation, Pittsburgh, Pennsylvania
1993
Plaster and vinyl paint
132 × 168 × 1 inch
Collection of the artist

20

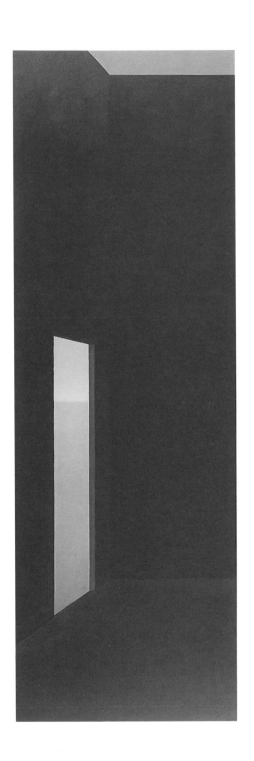

RED ROOM
1985
Oil on wood panel
72 × 24 inches

opposite
RUINS
1984
Oil and wax on canvas
96 × 96 inches
Collection of Mika Company,
Los Angeles

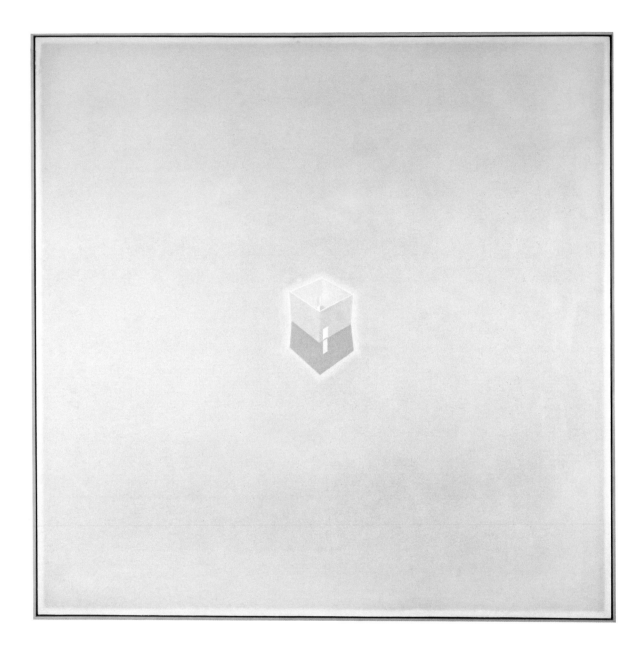

22

ROSE
1987
Oil and wax on canvas
84 × 84 inches
Collection of Tara Thomas, Los Angeles

TAUKIN
1986
Oil and wax on canvas
96 × 96 inches
Collection of Peter Mullins, Los Angeles

24

STEEL ROOM
1991
Stainless steel
8 × 8 × 8 inches
Collection of Nancy Kay,
Los Angeles

opposite
BLACK BRONZE ROOM
1991
Bronze
8 × 8 × 8 inches
Collection of Samuel & Barbara Masket,
Venice

26

UNTITLED
1991
Oil and wax on paper
40 × 30 inches
Collection of David Solzberg,
Los Angeles

opposite
LARGE VESSEL #2
1992
Oil and wax on canvas
96 × 60 inches
SunAmerica Collection,
Los Angeles

28

opposite
YIN AND YANG
1998
Oil on canvas
60 × 20 inches
Collection of Tricia Holland, Palo Alto, California

above
BLACK DOORS ON RED GROUND
1998
Oil on canvas
72 × 54 inches
Collection of Sue Wong and Dieter Raabe, Malibu

opposite
TIBETAN DOOR #1
1999
Oil on canvas
96 × 84 inches
Collection of Charles Thurston, Santa Monica

above
HANA
2000
Oil on canvas
72 × 54 inches
Collection of Mark Matheny, Los Angeles

according to rigid, uncompromising principles of efficient construction. These affordable, mass-produced buildings were rigid, corporate, and anonymous. Our everyday buildings—that familiar construction that defines the overwhelming majority of private homes and commercial spaces—are often bland and devoid of any sense of human necessity. Planned as a series of adaptable geometric units designed to accommodate any and all functions, they are appropriate for nothing in particular. As a result, these stark geometric spaces seem distant and indifferent.

Lodato's interiors—like the buildings we construct around us—are places of implied violence. Erecting a building requires an extreme reordering and disruption of the natural environment. Such spaces are alienating not only because they are inorganic, but also because they are uncompromising. Walls that are as thin as knife blades cut and cleave through space. Planes meet abruptly at harsh angles. Lodato exaggerated this implicit violence by distorting space within his rooms. By manipulating perspective he skewed space, compressing it at one end and expanding it at the other. Daniele Barbaro, an Italian Renaissance critic and artist, noted that when used improperly perspective becomes "strained, dizzily steep, deformed, or awkward."[10] These four defects are used to positive effect in Lodato's interiors. By placing his vanishing point closer to the viewer than normal, he succeeds in producing a feeling of abrupt convergence. The edges of his room rush off at wildly oblique angles, creating a sense of space that is at once more expansive and more claustrophobic than one might expect.

This conscious use of an unsettling interior calls to mind the work of Bruce Nauman. His famous corridors consist of interactive environments that coax the viewer to enter an uncomfortably narrow aisle. Nauman was Lodato's friend and neighbor when they both lived in Pasadena in the 1970s. The two share a concern with theatrical presentation. Like Nauman's corridors, Lodato's architectural fictions are intentionally unnerving. But where Nauman emphasized the self-referential and narcissistic qualities of the living body, Lodato has focused on lived space, particularly on the way space is self-consciously shaped and subdivided.

While Lodato's interiors seem centralized and unitary, they are actually governed by a powerful centrifugal energy. As in De Stijl painting and architecture—a movement to which Lodato stands as an indirect heir—an initial sense of classic harmony is soon dispelled by an expressionist pull to the edges. De Stijl art created images of a temporary balance and order from the harsh meeting of irreconcilable elements. In a similar manner, the center of one of Lodato's

33

opposite
RED AND BLACK
2000
Oil on canvas
96 × 68 inches
Collection of the artist

rooms appears as a void, held together tenuously by planes that threaten to move off in opposing directions.

Lodato saw the power of decentralization at work when he witnessed postwar suburban sprawl. When he was young, the region around his hometown of Van Nuys in the San Fernando Valley was rural. In the 1960s he saw it transformed by acre after acre of new housing developments. These bland, anonymous swaths of tract homes cut and divided the landscape. If first generation modernism was an urban art, then Lodato's work may be seen as a suburban art. It reflects the dislocation and decentering of the Postmodern, postindustrial world. Like the rhizomes postulated by Deleuze and Guattari, suburban developments spread in a haphazard, persistent and invasive manner. Lodato's fictive interiors carry a sense of acquiescence towards the anonymous forces that shape and control our world. If paintings such as *Ruins* and *Taukin* possess a feeling of transcendental peace, it must be remembered that this illusion of comforting quiet is conveyed by empty facades and false displays of security. It is no coincidence that Lodato's arresting and engaging interiors resemble Piranesi's eighteenth-century depictions of fantastic and picturesque prisons.

Lodato was able to invent such novel architectural interiors by freely moving and manipulating his perspective point. As he continued to play with these stage set designs, his viewpoint became more and more eccentric. By taking a bird's eye view he created paintings such as *Rose* (1987) as well as a series of three-dimensional sculptures. In *Rose*, the interior is seen from high above. From this voyeuristic vantagepoint, the entire room is made visible to the probing eye.

Lodato's sculpture clearly derives from his painted interiors. They resemble floorplans given actual height. The walls are angled with the widest part at top and the narrowest at the bottom. They appear to have been constructed from walls lying on the floor that have been tilted up to a point before they reach full vertical. The weight of the material gives these small sculptures a powerful presence. They are like fortresses, small self-contained dwellings. The walls are revealed for what they are—dense boundaries that shut off living space from everything outside.

Rooms open to the sky seem to elicit feelings of tranquil calm, of an environment free from threats of harsh weather. Yet these roofless enclosures are at the same time unsettling. They deny the primary quality we expect of housing—to provide shelter. Without a roof, these spaces are open and vulnerable. They offer a thick skin around the perimeter but this barrier is easily surmounted.

These constructed rooms depict dwellings as self-contained entities. Rather than depict arrangements of multiple rooms, Lodato chose to concentrate on a single, freestanding structure. The independent house is the American dream— the home to call one's own. Such separatism has become a condition of life in the late twentieth century. People strive for an absolute independence that inhibits contact with others, as seen in the proliferation of gated communities. These sculptures, which resemble elegant and sophisticated dollhouses, embody the American desire for both playful freedom and secure containment.

The sculptures reveal the room as a fortress-like bastion. In our culture the individual home is an icon. It is revered as a status symbol and a sanctified retreat. While Lodato was creating his illusionistic, three-dimensional interiors, he was also producing a series of rooms based on floorplans, as seen in *Untitled* (1991) and *Large Vessel #1* (1992). He even adopted this format for wall installations as seen in *Open Triangle*, an installation at the Mattress Factory in Pittsburgh (1993). These new compositions depict a floorplan seen from above, as if one were looking down into one of the room sculptures. A parallelogram in one corner stands for a door that admits light from an oblique angle. The resulting eccentric shape is formed from light falling upon the floor of the enclosed space.

Lodato often spoke of the open space in his art as a "void" or a "womb." While void denotes emptiness, womb signifies productivity, a realm of possibility. As in all his art, his Floorplan Abstractions are simultaneously empty and full. The light spilling into the room from a corner doorway spreads at an oblique angle, revealing a space that is intriguing but uncomfortable. As best seen in *Untitled* (1991), these interiors are literally edgy. Space is expansive and replete at the center, but crammed and distorted at the corners.

These flat abstract symbols address the same concerns as the illusionistic interiors but introduce a few new issues as well. A floorplan is a type of a map. These Floorplan Abstractions are about the mapping impulse, our tendency to delineate space into separate areas and regions. When the earliest cartographers first attempted to make sense of the land, they often mixed fact and fiction, creating imaginative and often fantastic explanations of regions unknown. Modern industrialized society, on the other hand, records space with factual precision. What cannot be rendered with mechanical, objective means is discounted as unimportant. Maps, groundplans, floorplans all attempt to define the outer boundaries of space, to describe area by recording external limits. In a similar way Lodato's Floorplan

Abstractions are highly compartmentalized. Each painting is a discrete and distinct unit, defined by clear borders. These paintings are condensed symbols of how we live in highly segregated and separated spaces.

Related to the Floorplan Abstractions are a series of Doorway Abstractions, featuring a monochrome field punctuated by four small rectangles or parallelograms. Each represents a door or portal. Typically, one rectangle is set in the middle of each edge of the canvas, as seen in *Black Doors on Red Ground* (1998). The placement of these doors has a pinwheel effect. These openings are governed by a centrifugal pull to the outer edges. In some works where the doors are rendered as parallelograms, the spiraling movement is more emphatic. The circular movement of a subtly spinning space creates a feeling of instability and flux, but also of fate.

Since the prehistoric era, time was linked to cycles of nature. The turnings of the day, season or year marked the passage of time and were regarded as signs of fate. In our culture spinning thread has long been a metaphor for destiny. Lodato's pinwheel rooms should be seen in this context, as places where fate is played out in our culture. The simplest domestic rooms often contain the most highly charged dramas of modern life. Hardly a neutral container, each room is a charged enclosure, enlivened and set in motion by the energy of everyday life. Lodato's Doorway Abstractions reveal the room as a complex sum of manifold energies.

After the Doorway Abstractions, Lodato saw the possibility of abandoning overt references to the room and began using just a few bars of color as spatial dividers. He created his latest and most recent series of paintings, consisting of a few vertical bands of two alternating colors. As seen in *Yin and Yang* (1998), where one white vertical band is paired with a parallel shape in black, these colors represent planes that open and close in space. His newest direction, which includes such spare but powerful abstractions as *Tibetan Door #1* (1999), *Hana* (2000), and *Red and Black* (2000), resulted from his desire to get back to the core of painting. As he explained, this new direction emerged when he "started to figure out what the essential parts of the painting were."[11] Lodato returned to the notion of art as a primarily visual experience. He used color to picture the space of painting.

Lodato's looming bands of color call to mind Mark Rothko's floating rectangles or Brice Marden's minimalist Grove Series, but with important differences. Rothko's paintings are uniformly atmospheric. He consistently employed a trembling edge around all forms to produce a feeling of anxious flux. Marden, on the other hand, made stolid, weighty paintings where each panel of opaque color formed a finite, independent unit. For Marden each color is a self-contained mass, resolute in its steadfast materiality. By contrast, Lodato used his bands of color to continue his life-long investigations into space. By subtly varying the quality of the edges, forms open into space or close down. Willem de Kooning once noted that when he painted his largest work, *Excavation* (1950), he conceived of the composition as an endless series of forms opening and then closing. Lodato engages in his own excavation of spatial perception, using color and edge to recreate the dynamics of human vision.

The surface of each stripe varies considerably. Some are dense and opaque, others are thin and airy. Image and surface breathe as one entity. The spatial sense they convey is best explained by the Japanese concept of "Ma." "Ma" refers to an active, vital space. Never conceived as a neutral emptiness, "Ma" is the living space around every physical thing. Lodato's bars of color convey this feeling through their sense of active unfolding. No element exists in isolation. Each bar of color plays an active role within a shifting field of fluid space.

Although emphatically abstract, these new paintings connect with the grand tradition of post-Renaissance representational painting. In 1975 Lodato discussed the essence of his wall installations in terms of a centuries-old Western tradition of visual illusion: "I think that the quality of magic has so much to do with the history of painting; of 'what's happening here?' It's in breaking something down and putting it back together, as in *Las Meninas* with all the different levels that that painting has—different levels of consciousness."[12]

While its external form differs dramatically from Velasquez's Baroque master-piece, a work such as *Tibetan Door #1* recreated the same spatial complexity. Subtly shifting bands of color refer to the human consciousness of interior space. The individual stripes are simultaneously barriers and openings. They can be seen as solid walls or open doors. As portals or obstacles they carry implications of shifting opportunities. Although these compositions are flat, airless and seemingly two-dimensional, they offer an emphatic assertion of pictorial space, and maintain the possibility that visual space still plays a role in abstract painting.

It is interesting to note that when Lodato first visited Japan he became fascinated by a museum of samurai swords. He was transfixed by these objects and considered them to be the highlight of his visit. These finely crafted swords captured his imagination because they contained within a single static form both profound violence and serene beauty. He praised these swords as representing a highly developed and refined art form, an art of such sophistication that it had internalized centuries of violence, turning it into sublimated objects of exquisite beauty. His recent paintings emulate this sense of aesthetic refinement, using sumptuous and finely worked planes of color to subsume and transcend the violence of everyday life.

Michael Zakian
Director
FREDERICK R. WEISMAN MUSEUM OF ART

1 Maurice Merleau-Ponty, *The Primacy of Perception* (Evanston, Il: Northwestern University Press, 1964), p. 166.

2 *Barnett Newman, Selected Writings and Interviews*, ed. by John O'Neill (Los Angeles: University of California Press, 1992), p. 111.

3 Francis Colpitt, *Peter Lodato: Dust* (exhibition catalogue), Baxter Art Gallery, California Institute of Technology, Pasadena, 1981, p. 14.

4 *Ibid*.

5 Melinda Wortz, *Peter Lodato* (exhibition catalogue), Fine Arts Gallery, University of California, Irvine, 1975, n.p.

6 William Wilson, "'The Wall': Not Just to Hang Pictures," *Los Angeles Times*, 27 February 1981, Part VI, p. 10.

7 Fidel Danieli, "Painterly Experiences," *Artweek*, 20 December 1975, pp. 5-6.

8 *Ibid*.

9 Wortz, n.p.

10 Daniele Barbaro, quoted in James Elkins, *The Poetics of Perspective* (Ithaca: Cornell University Press, 1994), p. 174.

11 Marina Walker, "Lit From Within," *Santa Barbara News-Press*, 4 April 1997, Scene section, p. 7.

12 Danieli, p. 5.

Underpaint

When an artist visits another artist in the studio, after some pleasantries and a look at what's before them, the talk often turns to how the object was made. Why isn't particularly interesting to artists. How is. It's a way of sharing, an intimacy. Why is a personal struggle; how is a common searching. Curators ask why. But why is elusive in the artist's mind. The why is in the work. That's what exhibitions are for: to examine the finished work of an artist.

Individual exhibitions give the clearest picture, or maybe I should say a clearer picture. Barnett Newman, an artist whose work Peter Lodato admires, once said that an artist spends his (or her) whole life on a single painting. If that is true, no picture is complete without all the work. Still, presenting an artist's work in the context of his or her own work rather than a broader context of art-makers, affords a sharper focus and perhaps a glimpse at why for that particular artist. It may be circumstantial, but it's right there on the surface.

What isn't in plain sight is the artist.

In 1988 Peter Lodato and I went to the first game of the season, "Opening Day" at Dodger Stadium. We've known each other for way more than twenty years. We are both LA natives, born six months apart, and longtime Dodger fans. The Dodgers lost, but we had a great time. At the end of that season, Kirk Gibson hit a huge home run and the Dodgers won the World Series.

What does this have to do with Peter Lodato's art? Probably not a whole lot. But it does have a lot to do with Peter.

I gave Peter's son Nicholas his first baseball when he was a few weeks old. Peter laughed and found some gloves so we could play catch in the street in front of his house. It was a total experience for Peter: emotional, physical, and aesthetic.

Maybe it does have something to do with his art.

I have a special relationship with Peter. I am an artist, and I have been a curator. And, we are friends. We share a deep interest in music, especially blues. As noted, we love sports. He's big and very strong and in college he was a fencer: emotional, physical, and aesthetic.

When I visit Peter in his studio, I get the experience of both a curator and an artist. I am often surprised by new turns in the work that are so obviously his own, yet unanticipated by me. Sometimes we talk about art history from Old Masters to Bob Irwin. We both lived for a time in Pasadena and share that rich heritage. I appreciate that Peter, in his role on the Artists Committee, helped our community learn from loss and build a lasting, vital institution in the Los Angeles Museum of Contemporary Art.

On a typical visit, there may be only two, three, or four finished works in the studio. More are in progress. Canvas and paper are stapled to walls, and he glows on and on about underpainting and overpainting and oil versus acrylic and texture, scale, and dimension. He says that this used to be like that and maybe that painting over there will be more red the next time I see it. There is always a great excitement in his voice as he shares the intimacy under the surface of his work: emotional, physical, aesthetic.

Michael H. Smith
Santa Barbara, 2000

Résumé

PETER LODATO

BORN   1946, Los Angeles, California

EDUCATION

1969-71
California State University, Northridge
Graduate studies in Art

1969
B.A., California State University, Northridge

TEACHING EXPERIENCE

1995-99 Art Center College of Design, Pasadena, California

1981-86 Otis/Parsons Art Institute, Los Angeles, California

1979-83 Art Center College of Design, Pasadena, California

1975-76 California Institute of the Arts, Valencia, California

1975 University of California, Irvine

AWARDS

1988 Brody Foundation Grant

1977 National Endowment for the Arts Grant

1975 National Endowment for the Arts Grant

SOLO EXHIBITIONS

2000
*Peter Lodato: From Painting to Installation, Selected Works,
1980 - 2000*
Frederick R. Weisman Museum of Art, Pepperdine
University, Malibu, California, catalogue

William Turner Gallery, Venice, California

1998
William Turner Gallery, Venice, California

1997
Handsel Gallery, Santa Fe, New Mexico

Manné Gallery, Santa Barbara, California

1996
William Turner Gallery, Venice, California

Open Studio, William Turner Gallery, Venice, California

1993
Special Projects - Installation
Mattress Factory, Pittsburgh, Pennsylvania

1991
Silver Tower, Public Art Project
Brunswig Square, Little Tokyo, Los Angeles, California

1990
Wrathful Means Project No. 2
Sharon Truax Fine Art, Venice, California

1989
Painting, Drawing & Sculpture
Hunsaker-Schlesinger Gallery, Los Angeles, California

1987
La Porta
Krygier/Landau Contemporary Art, Los Angeles,
California

1985
Angeline
Burnett Miller Gallery, Los Angeles, California

La Lune Noire
Hunsaker-Schlesinger Gallery, Los Angeles, California

La Mer
La Jolla Museum of Contemporary Art, La Jolla,
California

1982
Peter Lodato
Otis/Parsons Gallery, Los Angeles, California

China
Rosamund Felsen Gallery, Los Angeles, California

Peter Lodato
Aspen Center for the Visual Arts, Aspen, Colorado

1981
Mediation
Art Gallery of the Sibell-Wolle Fine Arts Building,
University of Colorado, Boulder, Colorado

Dust
California Institute of Technology, Pasadena,
California
catalogue

1980
Similarities and Opposites
Rosamund Felsen Gallery, Los Angeles, California

1978
Special Exhibition
Institute for Art and Urban Resources
Special Projects Room, P.S. 1, Queens, New York

1976
Peter Lodato
Minneapolis College of Fine Art and Design
Minneapolis, Minnesota

Sisters
Claire Copley Gallery, Los Angeles, California

1975
Peter Lodato
CARP, Roger Wong Studio, Los Angeles, California

Peter Lodato
Art Gallery, University of California, Irvine; catalogue

1973
Peter Lodato
Michael Walls Gallery, Los Angeles, California

1971
Peter Lodato
Brand Art Center, Glendale, California

SELECTED GROUP EXHIBITIONS
1999
Radical Past: Art and Music in Pasadena, 1960 – 1974
Armory Center for the Arts, Pasadena, California

1995
Charles Arnoldi, Kris Cox, Charles Hill, Peter
Lodato
William Turner Gallery, Venice, California

1992
Survey of California Art, 1960-90
Aspen Center for Visual Arts, Aspen, Colorado

1991
Salerno Incontrid-Arts
Rassegne della Ressegne Amalfi Arte, Salerno, Italy:
catalogue

1988
Sculpture Da Camera (Chamber Sculptures)
Fisher Gallery, University of Southern California

Vessels (Collaborative Exhibition)
Sharon Truax Fine Art and The Art Store Gallery,
Los Angeles, California

20th Century Watercolors: Yesterday and Today
Long Beach Museum of Art, Long Beach,
California

1987
America, America
4 Rassegna Internazionale d'Arte
Antichi Arsenali della Republica
Amalfi Arte, Amalfitana, Amalfi, Italy

1985
Peter Liashkov, Peter Lodato, Susan Rankaitis
Fisher Gallery, University of Southern California

New Ways of Seeing
Marilyn Pink/Master Prints and Drawings, Los
Angeles, California

1984
A Broad Spectrum
Design Center of Los Angeles

Contemporary Watercolors
Pink's Fine Art, Santa Monica, California

California Watercolors
California State University, San Diego, California

Reflections
Lonny Gans Gallery, Los Angeles, California

1983
Summer Show
Rosamund Felsen Gallery, Los Angeles, California

The Nancy Yewell Collection
Baxter Art Gallery
California Institute of Technology, Pasadena,
California; catalogue

Environs 2; Union Avenue
Art Gallery, Loyola School of Law, Los Angeles

Drawings by 50 California Artists
Modernism Gallery, San Francisco, California

1982
Painted Installations
80 Langston Street, San Francisco, California

1982 (continued)
New Work
Rosamund Felsen Gallery, Los Angeles, California

Rebounding Surface
Edith C. Bum Art Institute
Avery Center for the Arts
Bard College, Annandale-on-Hudson, New York

1981
1981 Biennial Exhibition
Whitney Museum of American Art, New York; catalogue

Nine and The Wall
Art Gallery, California State University, Fullerton

Decade: Los Angeles Painting in the Seventies
Art Center College of Design, Pasadena, California; catalogue

Group Show
Rosamund Felsen Gallery, Los Angeles

Forty Famous Californians: Recent Unique Works on Paper
Judith Christian Gallery, New York

7 form 703
Gensler and Associates/Architects, Los Angeles, California

1980
New Work
Rosamund Felsen Gallery, Los Angeles, California

1979
John McLaughlin, James Hayward, Peter Lodato
Los Angeles Institute of Contemporary Art
Christmas in July
Rosamund Felsen Gallery, Los Angeles, California

California Perceptions: Light and Space; Selections from the Wortz Collection
Art Gallery, California State University, Fullerton; catalogue

1977
100 Plus Directions in Southern California Art
Los Angeles Institute of Contemporary Art

Faculty Exhibition
School of Art and Design
California Institute of the Arts, Valencia, California; catalogue

1975
Eight Artists from L.A.
San Francisco Art Institute, San Francisco, California
Group Exhibition
Art Gallery, California State University, Los Angeles

1973
Group Exhibition
Leslie Collins Art Gallery, Dallas, Texas

Market Street Program: Nine Los Angeles Artists
San Francisco Museum of Art, San Francisco, California

Jerry Anderson, Greg Card, Laddie John Dill and Peter Lodato
Fine Art Gallery, California State University, Northridge

1972
Los Angeles: Fourteen Painters
Art Gallery, University of California, Santa Barbara

24 Los Angeles Artists
Los Angeles County Museum of Art

1970
Nine Artists
Fine Arts Gallery, University of California, Irvine

SELECTED COLLECTIONS

Bard College: Edith C. Blum Art Institute
Annandale-on-Hudson, New York

Syracuse University: Joe & Edith Lowe Art Gallery
Syracuse, New York

Brooklyn Museum, Brooklyn, New York

Seattle Art Museum, Seattle, Washington

Dallas Museum of Art, Dallas, Texas

College of Purchase, State University of New York:
Neuberger Museum, Purchase, New York

Hara Museum of Contemporary Art, Tokyo, Japan

BIBLIOGRAPHY

Michael Zakian, *Peter Lodato: From Painting to Installation, Selected Works, 1980–2000,*
Frederick R. Weisman Museum of Art, Pepperdine University, (exhibition catalogue), 2000.

Dottie Indyke, "Peter Lodato*," New Mexican Pasi Tiempo*, January 9, 1998.

Marina Walker, "Lit From Within," *Santa Barbara News*, April 4, 1997.

Allison Lee Solin, "Finding The Center," *The Independent*, April 3, 1997.

Peter Clothier, Los Angeles, (review of exhibition at Hunsaker/Schlesinger Gallery),
ArtNews, February 1990, p. 164.

Kenneth Baker, "Peter Lodato," La Jolla Museum of Contemporary Art, *Art
Forum*, November 1985, p. 114.

Frances Colpitt, "Peter Lodato at Burnett Miller Gallery in Los Angeles,"
Art in America, September 1985, p. 114.

Kristine McKenna, "Art Galleries," (review of exhibition at Burnett Miller Gallery), *Los
Angeles Times*, Part V, May 10, 1985.

Merl Shipper, "A Haven for Post-Modernism," *Artweek*, May 25, 1985.

Suzanne Muchnic, "New Listing: Four Rooms with a View" (review of exhibition at

Otis/Parsons), *Los Angeles Times,* Calendar, February 10, 1982.

Robert L. Pincus, "Galleries," *Los Angeles Times*, Calendar, April 16, 1982

Ralph C. Bond, "On and Off the Wall," *Artweek*, March 7, 1981, p. 5.

Lora Pethik Brown and Jane Cope Pence, *Nine and the Wall*, California State University, Fullerton Art Gallery, Fullerton, California, 1981.

Flora Cater, "Peter Lodato's Meditation at UC Boulder," *Artspace: Southwestern Contemporary Arts Quarterly*, Fall 1981, p. 66.

Robert Hughes, "Quirks, Clamour and Variety," *Time Magazine*, Vol. 117, No. 9, March 2, 1981, p. 84.

Christopher Knight, "A Decade of L.A. Painting Crammed into One Exhibition," *Los Angeles Herald Examiner*, March 8, 1981, Part E, p. 7.

Mark Johnstone, "Exploration and Installation," *Artweek*, October 24, 1981, page 5.

Suzanne Muchnic, "Odd Couple Interested in Illusion," *Los Angeles Times*, Calendar, October 4, 1981, page 91.

John Perrault, "A Singular Pluralism," *The Soho News*, February 11, 1981, page 27.

Whitney Museum of American Art, *Biennial Exhibition*, New York, 1981.

William Wilson, "The Wall, Not Just to Hang Pictures," *Los Angeles Times*, February 27, 1981, Part VI, page 10.

William Wilson, "A Cocktail Party of the Second Kind," *Los Angeles Times*, Calendar, March 1, 1981, page 80.

Melinda Wortz, "Abstract Painting in Los Angeles 1950-1980: Selections from the Murray and Ruth Gribin Collection," *Journal: A Contemporary Arts Magazine*, September-October, 1981.

Richard Armstrong, "California," *Flash Art*, March-April, 1980, pp. 30-31.

Hunter Drohojowska, "Artbeat: Peter Lodato's Sensitivity to the Inobvious," *L.A. Weekly,* January 18-24, 1980.

Adrienne Rosenthal, "The Illumination of Seeing," *Artweek*, January 2, 1980, pp. 1, 20.

William Wilson, "Review," *Los Angeles Times*, January 26, 1980.

Joseph E. Young, "Artist's Paintings go Beyond the Edge of the Canvas," *The Arizona Republic,* January 20, 1980.

Michael Kurcfeld, "Visible Means of Support," *New West*, October 9, 1979, vol. 3, no. 21, p.106.

Susan Larsen, "Where Conceptual Meets Perceptual," *Artnews*, January 1979, pp. 94, 96.

Melinda Wortz, *California Perceptions: Light and Space, Selections from the Wortz Collection*, Fullerton Art Gallery, Fullerton, California, 1979.

Faculty Exhibition, California Institute of the Arts, Valencia, California, 1977.

William Wilson, "Irvine Exhibits Lodato, Pashgian," *Los Angeles Times*, December 22, 1975, Part IV, pp. 6-7.

Fidel Danieli, "Painterly Experiences," *Artweek*, 20 December 1975, pp. 5–6.

Melinda Wortz, *Peter Lodato*, University of California, Irvine, 1975.

Elena Canavier, "Peter Lodato: Wall Works," *Artweek*, February 24, 1973, Vol. 4, No. 8, pp. 1, 12.

Fidel Danieli, "Objects as Infinite Space," *L.A. Weekly News*, 1973, Part IV, p. 4.

Barbara Hansen, "Hamburgers Feature a Satiric Bite," *Los Angeles Times*, July 1, 1971, Part IV, p. 1.

April Kingsley, "Los Angeles," *The Art Gallery*, Summer 1971, pp. 21, 74.

Hilton Kramer, "Los Angeles: Now the 'In' Art Scene," *New York Times*, June 1, 1971, p. 21.

Maurice Tuchman and Jane Livingston, *24 Los Angeles Artists*, Los Angeles County Museum of Art, Los Angeles, 1971.

William Wilson, "Two Shows Give Southlanders a Broad Look at What's New," *Los Angeles Times*, Calendar, June 13, 1971, p. 48.

SELECTED ART CRITICISM BY THE ARTIST:

Michael Asher, Documenta 5, Kassel, West Germany, 1972.

"Three Los Angeles Sculptors: Lloyd Hamrol, George Herms, Bruce Nauman," catalogue statement for exhibition at The Los Angeles Institute of Contemporary Art, September 16 to October 24, 1975, published in *Journal, A Contemporary Arts Magazine*, No. 8, November –December 1975, pp. 50-57.

Lenders to the exhibition

Nurit and Ichak Adizes

The Capital Group Foundation

Jon and Janice Jerde

Nancy Kay

Hannah and Russel Kully

Peter Lodato

Barbara and Samuel Masket

Mark Matheny

Mika Company, Los Angeles

Edith Morgan

Jayme Odgers

Adrian and Constance Saxe

Carl and Judy Schlosberg

Frank Schweitzer

SunAmerica Collection, Los Angeles

Tamara and Hardy Thomas

Tara Thomas

Tatyana Thompson

Sue Wong and Dieter Raabe

Acknowledgements

An exhibition of this complexity could not have been undertaken without the help of numerous individuals who all deserve my thanks.

It was a true privilege to work closely with Peter Lodato. He warmly opened his studio to me, enduring numerous visits, nagging questions and innumerable phone calls. One of the joys of curating exhibitions of living artists is having the chance to get close to an artist's work and vision. The greatest compliment I can pay Peter is to say that I learned much from working with him. I hope that this exhibition and my catalogue essay do his art justice.

Second only to Peter's personal involvement is the work done by artist and graphic designer, Jayme Odgers. I owe Jayme a debt of gratitude for the exceptional designs he produced for the exhibition catalogue, invitation and banner. His skill as a designer and sensitivity to Peter's art resulted in a beautiful publication. In addition, he oversaw catalogue production from beginning to end.

I would like to thank the lenders, listed on the preceding page, who agreed to part with their art so that it can be shared with the public. Peter's collectors form a loyal group who enthusiastically supported this venture from the start. Their willingness to lend their art to this exhibition is commendable.

The catalogue was underwritten by many people who believe in Peter's art. Special appreciation is owed to the select individuals and companies, listed on a following page, who made contributions to help cover the costs of this publication. Additional funding was provided by the Frederick R. Weisman Art Foundation.

Curator and artist Michael H. Smith kindly wrote a personal reflection inspired by his decades-long friendship with Peter. His words offer a picture of the artist as a human being and add another dimension to the art on view.

For this exhibition, Peter agreed to create a monumental wall painting entitled *JOTT (The High Window)* in the majestic Gregg G. Juarez Gallery within the

Frederick R. Weisman Museum of Art. Measuring twenty-five feet high and fifty-two feet wide, this site-specific painting presented many logistical problems. I wish to thank Keith Rodabaugh for helping the artist fabricate Sheetrock panels. I would also like to thank Michael C. Johnson and Pepperdine University's painting crew for their professionalism and skill in helping execute this project.

At Pepperdine University's Center for the Arts, I want to thank Stewart O'Rourke and Marc Shroetter for their expert installation of the exhibition. Linda Ball provided valuable clerical support. Brad Cope oversaw publicity. As always, Marnie Mitze offered enthusiastic support for this project.

Lastly, I would like to dedicate this exhibition and catalogue to Andrew K. Benton as he embarks on his first year as seventh president of Pepperdine University.

Checklist for the Exhibition

STUDY FOR INSTALLATION WITH WAXED FLOOR
1980
Watercolor and gouache on paper
26 × 21 1/2 inches
Collection of Edith Morgan

ROUGE
1981
Oil on canvas
36 × 36 inches
Collection of Hannah & Russel Kully

RUINS
1984
Oil and wax on canvas
96 × 96 inches
Collection of Mika Company, Los Angeles

UNTITLED
1984
Watercolor on paper
60 × 40 inches
Collection of Sue Wong

ZUIKAN
1985
Oil and wax on canvas over panel
96 × 96 inches
Collection of The Capital Group Foundation

STUDY FOR TAUKIN
1986
Watercolor on paper
10 × 10 inches
Collection of Jayme Odgers

UNTITLED
1986
Oil on gold leaf on mylar
24 × 32 inches
Collection of Tatyana Thompson

ROSE
1987
Oil and wax on canvas
84 × 84 inches
Collection of Tara Thomas

BLACK BELL
1989
Bronze
10 1/2 × 10 1/2 × 9 1/2 inches
Collection of Adrian and Constance Saxe

GOLDEN ROOM
1989
Polished bronze
7 × 7 × 7 inches
Collection of Carl and Judy Schlosberg

STAINLESS STEEL ROOM
1989
Stainless steel
8 × 8 × 8 inches
Collection of Nancy Kay

BLACK BRONZE ROOM
1991
Cast bronze
8 × 8 × 8 inches
Collection of Barbara and Samuel Masket

CAST IRON ROOM
1991
Cast iron
8 × 8 × 8 inches
Collection of Jon and Janice Jerde

LARGE VESSEL #2
1992
Oil and wax on canvas over panel
96 × 60 inches
SunAmerica Collection, Los Angeles

UNTITLED
1993
Oil on canvas
10 × 8 inches
Collection of Tamara and Hardy Thomas

SMALL VESSEL #2
1994
Oil on canvas
10 × 8 inches
Collection of Adrian and Constance Saxe

BLACK & WHITE
1996
Oil on canvas
14 × 11 inches
Collection of Frank Schweitzer

MY RUSSIAN FAMILY
1997-98
Oil on canvas
72 × 54 inches
Collection of Nurit and Ichak Adizes

BLACK DOORS ON RED GROUND
1999
Oil on canvas
72 × 54 inches
Collection of Sue Wong and Dieter Raabe

TIBETAN DOOR #2
1999
Oil on canvas
96 × 84 inches
Collection of the artist

BLACK AND RED
2000
Oil on canvas
96 × 68 inches
Collection of the artist

HANA
2000
Oil on canvas
72 × 54 inches
Collection of Mark Matheny

TMT
2000
Oil on gold leaf on Mylar
25 × 20 inches
Collection of Tatyana Thompson

VIOLET AND GOLDEN YELLOW
2000
Oil on linen
40 × 30 inches
Collection of the artist

installation

JOTT (THE HIGH WINDOW)
2000
Flashe vinyl paint, Sheetrock,
joint compound and powdered
pigment
299 × 640 inches
Collection of the artist

This exhibition has been organized by
the Frederick R. Weisman Museum of Art,
Pepperdine University, Malibu, California.

October 14—December 15, 2000

Funding for the exhibition is provided by the
Frederick R. Weisman Art Foundation.
Funding for the exhibition catalogue is provided
by the Frederick R. Weisman Art Foundation
and the following contributors:

Nurit and Ichak Adizes

Bente and Gerald E. Buck

The Capital Group Foundation

Charlotte Chamberlain and Paul Weiselmann

Sandra Kulli and Dundas I. Flaherty

Hannah and Russel Kully

Mika Company

John Morton and Laura Donnelley-Morton

Peggy Phelps

William and Deborah Richards

Scott Schwartz

SunAmerica, Los Angeles

Geoffrey and Reba Thomas

Photography Credits

Brian Forrest
Black Doors on Red Ground, Hana, Red and Black, Tibetan Door #1, Yin and Yang

Nancy Hirsh
Otis/Parsons Installation

Jayme Odgers
Four Studies for Installations, La Mer (drawing)*, Zuikan*
Portrait of Peter Lodato, p. 6, and p. 39

Robert Seidemann
Ruins

Linda Shaffer
Portrait of Peter Lodato, p. 2–3

David Solzberg
Large Vessel #1, Red Room, Steel Room, Untitled (1991)

Catalogue © 2000. All rights reserved.
Frederick R. Weisman Museum of Art, Pepperdine University

All artwork © 2000 Peter Lodato.

Catalogue designed by Jayme Odgers, Los Angeles, California
Typeset in Bembo with Futura Bold headings
Printed by Typecraft, Pasadena, California

ISBN 1-882705-02-5